A New Beginning

Kayla Kimball

A publication of

Eber & Wein Publishing

Pennsylvania

A New Beginning

Library of Congress
Cataloging in Publication Data

ISBN 978-1-60880-509-9

Proudly manufactured in the United States of America by

Eber & Wein Publishing
Pennsylvania

Contents

Friendship Court

Friendship Court is wonderful
Friendship Court is great
Friendship Court is number one
In Minnesota State

The help is very special
The residents the same
A smile is on all faces
Come and join the game

The staff is always busy
Making sure we're fine
If we need or want
They always have the time

I am very happy
They had room for me
Otherwise I know
I'd be somewhere up a tree

A Day at Friendship Court

Breakfast is at seven
For those who want to eat
Those who come later
Will also get a seat

Coffee is at ten
If you don't get enough
Lunch is at eleven
To eat until you're stuffed

Then there is coffee
Between two and three
After that is supper
If you are still hungry

When you're done eating
There are things to do
There are playing cards and bingo
To name just a few

There are many kinds of trivia
And Bible study too
There is laughing and talking
Between me and you

If you have a problem
And don't want to be alone
Please come and make
Friendship Court your home

When You Get Up

When you get up in the morning
Say a little prayer
Thank our God for keeping you
Through a nighttime of despair

Remember He is with you
Anywhere you go
He will always guide you
Because He loves you so

Don't give up on Jesus
He is always there
He will always love you
No matter when or where

When you're feeling down
And don't know where to turn
Know that Jesus loves you
The midnight light will burn

A Purpose

Each life has a purpose
Each purpose a plan
Great minds find a reason
To do what they can

A hope for tomorrow
A task for today
Through troubles or sorrow
Each trial on life's way

A purpose for living
A test you must meet
Accepting each challenge
The bitter, the sweet

Cast aside every problem
Rise above endless fears
Keep the dream you are dreaming
Wipe away hurtful tears

Understanding—forgiveness
A soul that knows peace
The joy of believing
As heartaches then cease

The courage that's needed
To travel each mile
A purpose unequaled
A life that's worthwhile

God Cares

When life gets you down
With its troubles and cares
And you're tossed by the waves
And the winds of the air

You need only to look
At the places you've been
The storms and the trials
And the days with no end

For they each will remind you
How you made it through
And each will bring hope
And comfort too

For God's care is for always
Not just now and then
Each yesterday and tomorrow
And each day my friend

God Can Make a Way

When disappointment fills your heart
And doubt invades your mind
Count your many blessings
And hopefully you'll find

That even when your heart aches
God's hand is on your life
He walks with you in good times
He carries you through strife

I know this time is trying
And I pray for you today
But I hope you will remember
That God will make the way

A Word of Kindness

A word of kindness lasts all day
To light another's heart and way
And if we add a caring smile
It adds a joy to traveled miles

A simple word of kindly care
Or just a smile to ease despair
For Jesus preached in days on Earth
That we respect each other's birth

And love each other in His name
Who live and pray and die the same
And when the time to home we go
We will be happy; this I know

When Daylight Fades

When daylight fades and nighttime comes
And earlier gets dark
We know that winter's right behind
And it will leave its mark

We know that it will soon get cold
And we will have to stay
In our house so cuddly warm
And not go out to play

Soon the snow will be here
The ice not far behind
The days will get so very long
And be anything but kind

The nighttime will be longer
And never seem to end
We will pace the floor
And pray that God will send

Someone to come and help
Take the snow away
So we won't have to be
In the house more than a day

The Leaves Are Changing Color

The leaves are changing colors
And fall is in the air
We know what lies ahead
The trees will soon be bare

We know it will get cold
And snow is soon to come
We want time to slow down
But it is on the run

Hurry, hurry, hurry
Is what the wind does say
Slow down, slow down, way down
Is how I feel today

The Hour I Treasure Most

The hour I treasure most
Is when the day is new
Before the rush comes crowding in
With tasks that I must do

As I humbly kneel in prayer
All fears and worries cease
There is no other time I know
That brings this inner peace

I ask His guidance for my day
On pathways old and new
That I'll be kind to those I meet
In all I say and do

And should it seem that no one cares
And I am feeling blue
It's then I hear His voice so sweet
"My child, I love you"

When the day draws to a close
I give thanks for all that's been
And ask that He'll keep watch o'er me
Till morning comes again

No need have I for counting sheep
I'm in the shepherd's care
What peace is ours when we begin
And end each day with prayer

God Can Move Your Mountain

When things seem so impossible
And life's so hard to bear
God can move your mountain
Before you reach despair

He'll never leave you or forsake you
Trust Him all the way
Be anxious, then, for nothing
And never cease to pray

So keep on climbing higher
Be patient while you wait
For God is never early
And also never late

Today Is November

Today is November
Two thousand fifteen
The weather is wonderful
More like a dream

It has been wonderful
All fall long
It makes me want
To sing a song

I know it won't stay
And soon it will be
Snow flying fast
And we cannot see

We must enjoy it
While it is here
Hip hip hooray
Let's all give a cheer

Cloudy it's been
Once in a while
But here comes the sun
Again we can smile

A little rain comes
Now and then
It could be snow
Once again

Tomorrow the weather
Will change in a flash
And our good weather
Is a thing of the past

What Are You Thankful For?

What are you thankful for
This Thanksgiving Day?
What are you thinking
As you kneel down to pray?

Is it for family
And also for friends?
Is it for what
May be 'round the bend?

We never know
What lies ahead
Go to my Father
As once Jesus said

He will take care
Of you every day
If you remember
To kneel down and pray

Happy Thanksgiving

Whisper of Winter

There's a whisper of winter
This November day
While tiny white snowflakes
Now fall on our way

Clouds high above
Are wearing a frown
And winter is dressed
In a frosty white gown

There's a whisper of winter
In sharp winds that blow
And stars in the heavens
Are now hanging low

Little creatures now scurry
To find warmth and cheer
They know without question
That winter is here

The earth is now frozen
The garden asleep
The season of winter
A promise to keep

There's a smile bright golden
From last rays of sun
While a whisper of winter
Lends moments of fun

Lord, Please Remind Me

Lord, please remind me
Of promises made in prayer
I said if You relieve me
Of burdens that I bear

I always would be trusting
And my faith would never stray
I'd know You walk beside me
Every hour of the day

But, Lord, I'm only human
And should burdens reappear
I may forget I promised
To trust You without fear

Again, please, Lord, remind me
I made a sacred vow
To never doubt Your goodness
Lord, please remind me now

Today We Honor Heroes

Today we honor heroes
Who answered our country's call
We must never forget
We must remember all

Those who are gone
And those who still remain
We must honor all
Who helped us through the pain

There were many good times
There were many bad
Some were very happy
Many were very sad

When we meet a hero
We must always say
Thank you for giving me
The life we have today

Today Is Pearl Harbor Day

Today is Pearl Harbor Day
In nineteen forty-one
The Japanese attacked us
And war had just begun

We must remember
Those who went to war
And gave up their lives
For us forevermore

Germany declared
War the next day
World War II was started
And in it we did stay

Many lost their lives
And loved ones went on alone
We must remember
The ones who never came home

The Greatest Gift

The greatest gift at Christmastime
Is one we all may give
A friendly smile that helps to make
Life easier to live

A kindly thought, a helping hand
To show someone we care
And let them know how much it means
For us to have them there

The greatest gift at Christmastime
Costs not a lot to buy
It's being a good neighbor
As days and months go by

It's offering a shoulder
When someone needs a lift
And so I pray this Christmas Day
That this may be your gift

I Love to Watch the Christmas Lights

I love to watch the Christmas lights
Shining on the tree
Knowing God sent His son
To die for you and me

Forget the endless shopping
And focus on His birth
Jesus came to save
A sinful fallen Earth

This Christmas let us worship Him
And spend our time in prayer
Offering God our thankfulness
For His guidance and His care

May God's presence fill your heart with love
And cast out every fear
May you have a blessed Christmas
And a peaceful, safe New Year

I Love the Christmas Season

I love the Christmas season
To me it is so grand
The spirit of joyous giving
Breaks forth across this land

Some don't even understand
Why at this time of year
They have a special tenderness
For all whom they hold dear

Could it be within their hearts
Our Lord has entered in
And maybe briefly at this time
Their thoughts have turned to Him

Please let it be, dear Savior
This prayer I pray is true
That many at this time of year
Will give their hearts to You

Gather Your Christmas Dreams

Take time to gather your Christmas dreams
At this beautiful time of year
You'll find so much to treasure, to keep
Along with your Christmas cheer

A faith and hope that lives in your heart
As Jesus would enter your mind
Goodness and mercy forever your own
With all of life's worry behind

Gather the star shine to gladden your soul
The blessings from Heaven above
All of the magic the season can bring
God's precious caring and love

Mistletoe, holly, a tree standing tall
And children you hold ever dear
Your own Christmas angel to lend you peace
This holy time of the year

Merry Christmas, God's blessings to you and to yours
And after the holiday's done
Continue to gather your Christmas dreams
Through the new year and each one to come

Home at Christmastime

It isn't far to home sweet home
When Christmas sights we see
For we can always travel there
Though snowbound we may be

Though winds may blow the snowdrifts high
And bitter cold may reign
That going home for Christmas
Will in our hearts remain

It is not far to that dear spot
Where family ties still live
There's still a way to home sweet home
Where treasured joys are hid

For thoughts and hearts can travel there
No distance can erase
The going home at Christmastime
Back to the old home place

Thank You to Santa

Thank you to Santa
Who came to Friendship Court
Who left us the goodies
For us to sort

To eat if we want
Or maybe give away
We wish you had come
To stay for the day

Thanks anyway
For the love you did show
We appreciate all
And want you to know

Another Year Is Dawning

Another year is dawning
With the chance to start anew
May I be kinder, wiser, Lord
In all I say and do

The warm, kind word that I can give
The outstretched hand to help
The prayers I pray for those in need
More precious these than wealth

I know not what may lie ahead
Of laughter or of tears
I only need to know each day
That You are walking near

I'm thankful for this brand new year
As now I humbly pray
My hand secure in Yours, dear Lord
Each step along the way

A Listening Heart

Dear Lord, I want a listening heart
Not only ears that hear
For only when I listen well
Your presence feels so near

I want my eyes to see much more
Not just a small, small part
For eyes may not reveal as much
Seen by a loving heart

My lips may speak so many words
But they may be in vain
The listening heart is open to
Another's grief and pain

There's so much pain and sorrow, Lord
I need to feel You near
Just give me words and eyes that see
And, Lord, a heart that hears

I thank You for Your loving care
And, Lord, I humbly pray
For love enough to pass along
To those along life's way

Perhaps they need some "comfort" words
But that is only part
So in the quiet of the hour
I want a listening heart

A Loving Heart

A loving heart, an endearing smile
A warm and gentle touch
We give so many things in life
But nothing means as much

A little inspiration
When someone loses hope
A kind word of encouragement
When they no longer cope

A simple phrase, *I love you*
When no one else is there
Taking hold of a hand
In a loving heartfelt prayer

Love is never silent
It has so much to say,
And it is our great blessing
When we give it all away

Heart to Heart

Somewhere a heart is drowning
In tears it tries to hide
Let not your eyes be blinded
To its false display of pride

Somewhere a heart keeps reaching
For dreams that fade and die
Let not your ears be deafened
To its sad and mournful cry

Take time to look and listen
You will find each broken heart
And to show an act of kindness
God will bless you for your part

Thank You to All

Thank you to all
That help every day
To make our life here
Much more like play

You're friendly and kind
And do so much more
Than I was told
When I came through the door

You clean and serve meals
You give me a ride
There's always a smile
On the outside

Thank you so much
I'm glad that I came
To Friendship Court
To join in the game

Thank you all for taking the time
To read this book although it's mine
I write for all I like so much
And also those I want to touch

I hope my words do much for you
To make your day enjoyable too
When you read this, think of me
Let me know what I should see

Are you rich or are you poor?
I don't need to know anymore
Do you love God or is that wrong?
Am I where I don't belong?

God is my Maker, this I know
I want to share with all I know
If in Him you do believe
He will take care of you in need

CPSIA information can be obtained at www.ICGtesting.com
Printed in the USA
BVOW08s0550050716

454194BV00001B/19/P